BY JOY NAGY

HARRY N. ABRAMS, INC. PUBLISHERS, NEW YORK

A REGINA RYAN BOOK

INSTRUCTIONS

The letters take form through a simple process of scoring, cutting, folding, and gluing. It is important to take your time. First, study the pieces of the letter to understand how they fit together. Trace the outlines of any letters you may wish to duplicate. Then, slowly go through the steps outlined below. If you make a wrong cut, use invisible tape on the back to mend the paper. Glue no more than two inches at a time, so that you can correct any mistake before the glue sets.

TOOLS NEEDED:

For scoring: The dull edge of a dinner knife or
A metal ruler or one with a metal edge

For cutting: Scissors. A pair with a sharp point is useful for cutting out the smaller holes in the letters. Cuticle scissors are useful for cutting round edges
An X-acto or similar craft knife. Use it with a ruler for straight edges

For folding: The ruler or your fingernail to sharpen the edges of the folds

For gluing: White glue
Toothpicks to spread the glue evenly and to get into small spaces

For stabilizing the letters with a small base (C, F, I, J, P, T):
Several coins (like eight pennies) per letter, or dried beans or similar weights. Using different objects will produce a variety of sounds when the letters are shaken

For manipulating pieces: Tweezers may be useful

SYMBOLS:

Solid gray lines: Cut these lines
Broken lines: Score these lines
Gray triangles: Score between the points of the triangles, and fold IN
White triangles: Score between the points of the triangles and fold OUT
Dots: Connect pieces at these points. Connect one dot to one dot, two dots to two dots, and so on
Star: Start assembling here

STEP-BY-STEP INSTRUCTIONS:

1. Remove the page with the letter pattern from the book. Cut at the very edge of the binding, where indicated.
2. Score all pieces where indicated *before* you cut out each piece.
3. Cut out the pieces. It is best to cut the whole piece out first, and then cut out the notches and smaller indentations. Cut at the very edge of the design.
4. Fold the white tabs and corners. Go over the folds with the ruler or your fingernail to make them crisp and sharp.
5. Glue the long strips together, matching the dots on the tabs. This will give you a continuous band that will form the outer shape of the letter. On certain letters (A, B, C, D, G, O, P, Q, R), there will also be interior strips. These strips should be glued together as well, matching dot to dot. *Use glue sparingly.*
6. Fold the strips into the form of the letter. The star on the strip indicates where to

begin your series of folds. For those strips that form curves, it is best to hold the strip at each end and slide gently against the edge of a table. This will create a slight curl in the paper and make it more flexible. The curl should go in the same direction as the curve of the letter.

7. Glue the outer strip to the flat letter shape to create the back and outer sides of the letter. Put a few drops of glue on the tabs, enough to cover about two inches at a time. Spread the glue with a toothpick. Press the tab onto the letter shape. Work slowly, doing small portions at a time. Line up the edges carefully. Continue this process until the back and outer edge of your letter are in place and joined.

8. Place the inner strip in position in the center of the letter, with the design facing out. Glue the inner strip into place.

9. Attach the front of the letter just as you did the back. NOTE: Before you do this with the letters with slender bases—C, F, I, J, P, T—place 8 pennies (or other items of similar weight) in the bottom of each. This is the magic trick that allows these letters to defy gravity, but you can place them in other letters also.

EXAMPLE:

After you have scored and cut out all your pieces:

1. Glue the two outer strips together, matching single dots to single dots and double dots to double dots. The result will be one continuous band
2. Fold this band into the shape of the letter A
3. Glue the band to the inside of the flat letter
4. Glue the interior strip to form one continuous band, making sure the pattern faces outward
5. Fold the interior band
6. Glue the interior band into the center of the letter
7. Glue the front of the letter into place

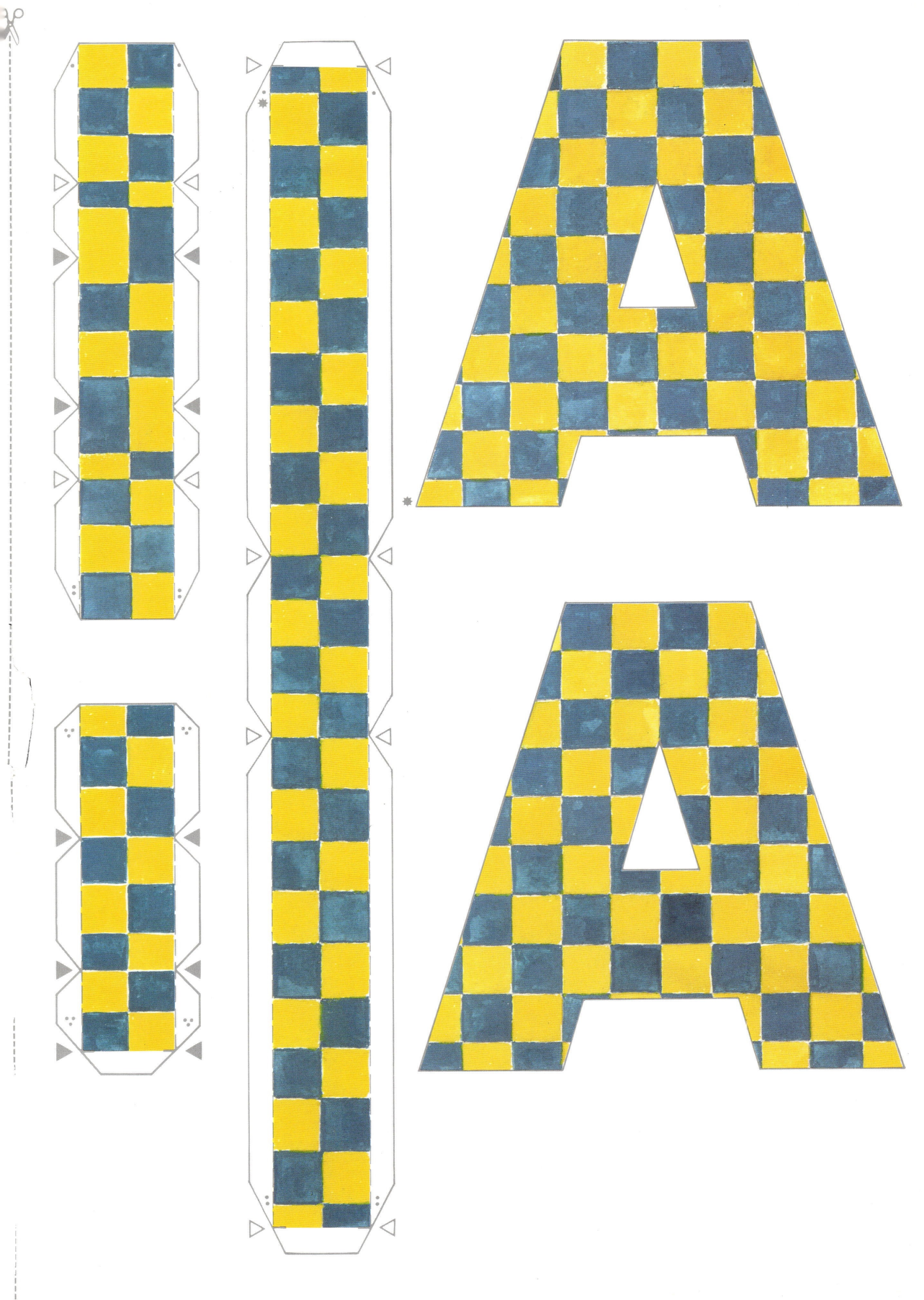

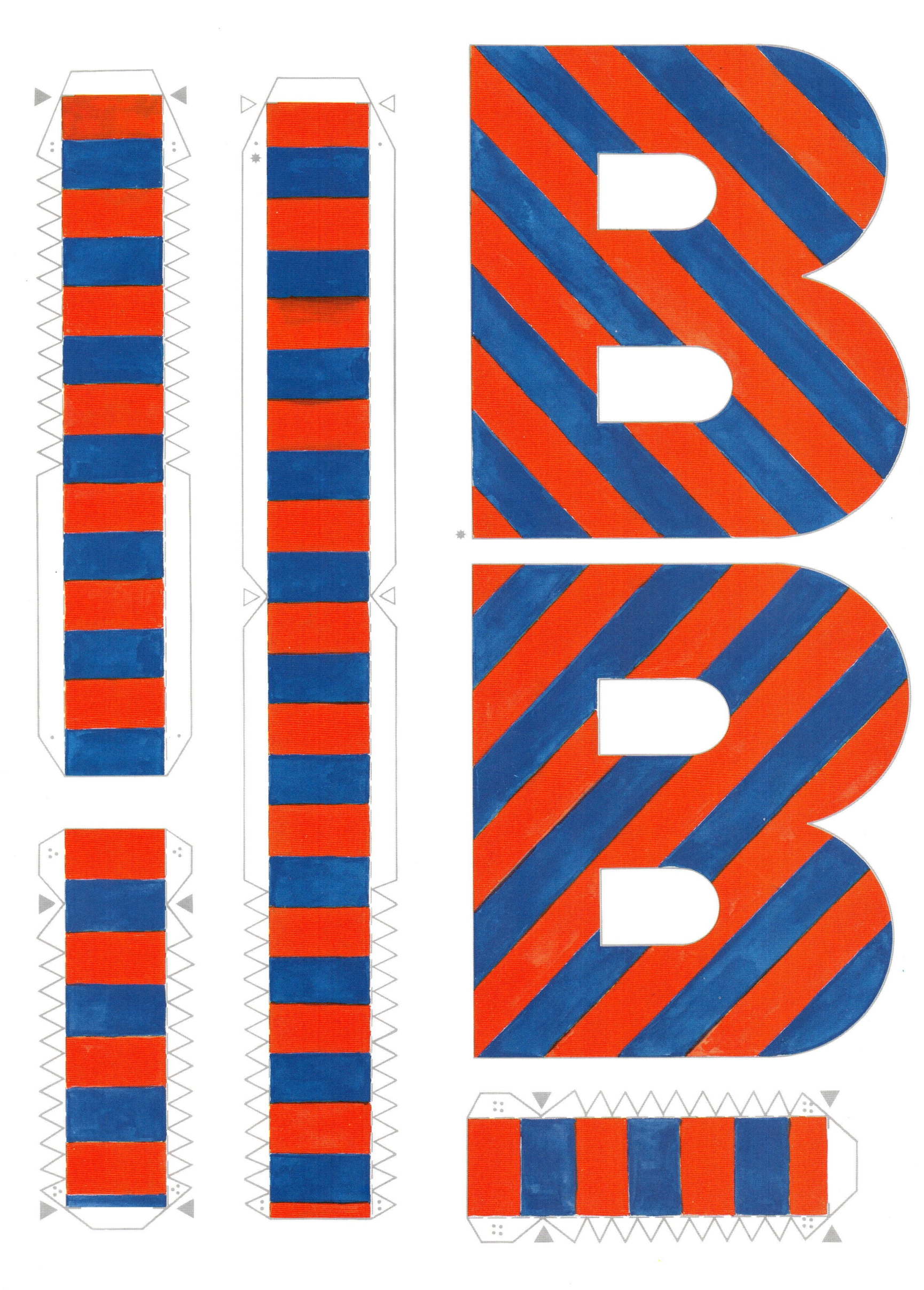

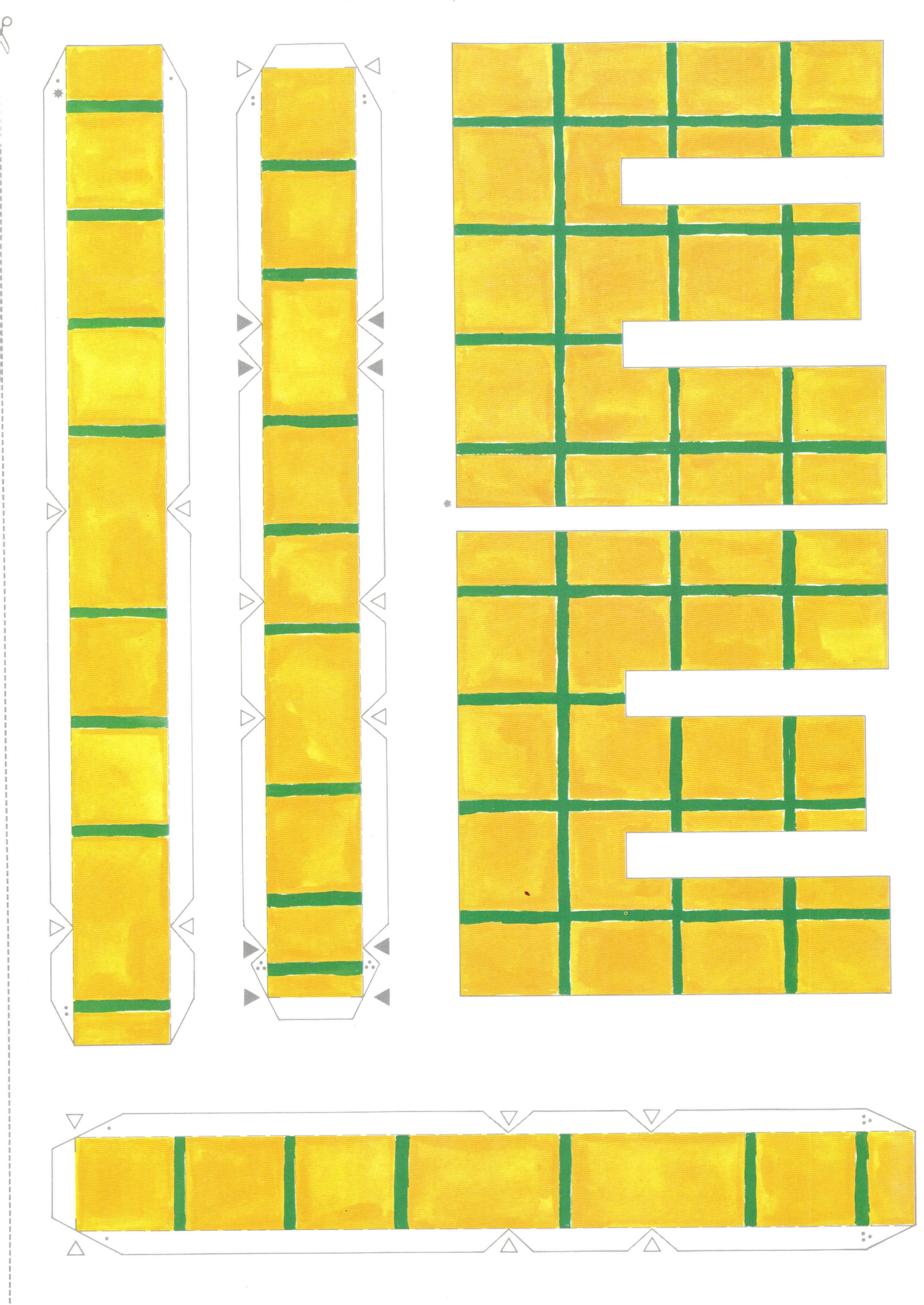

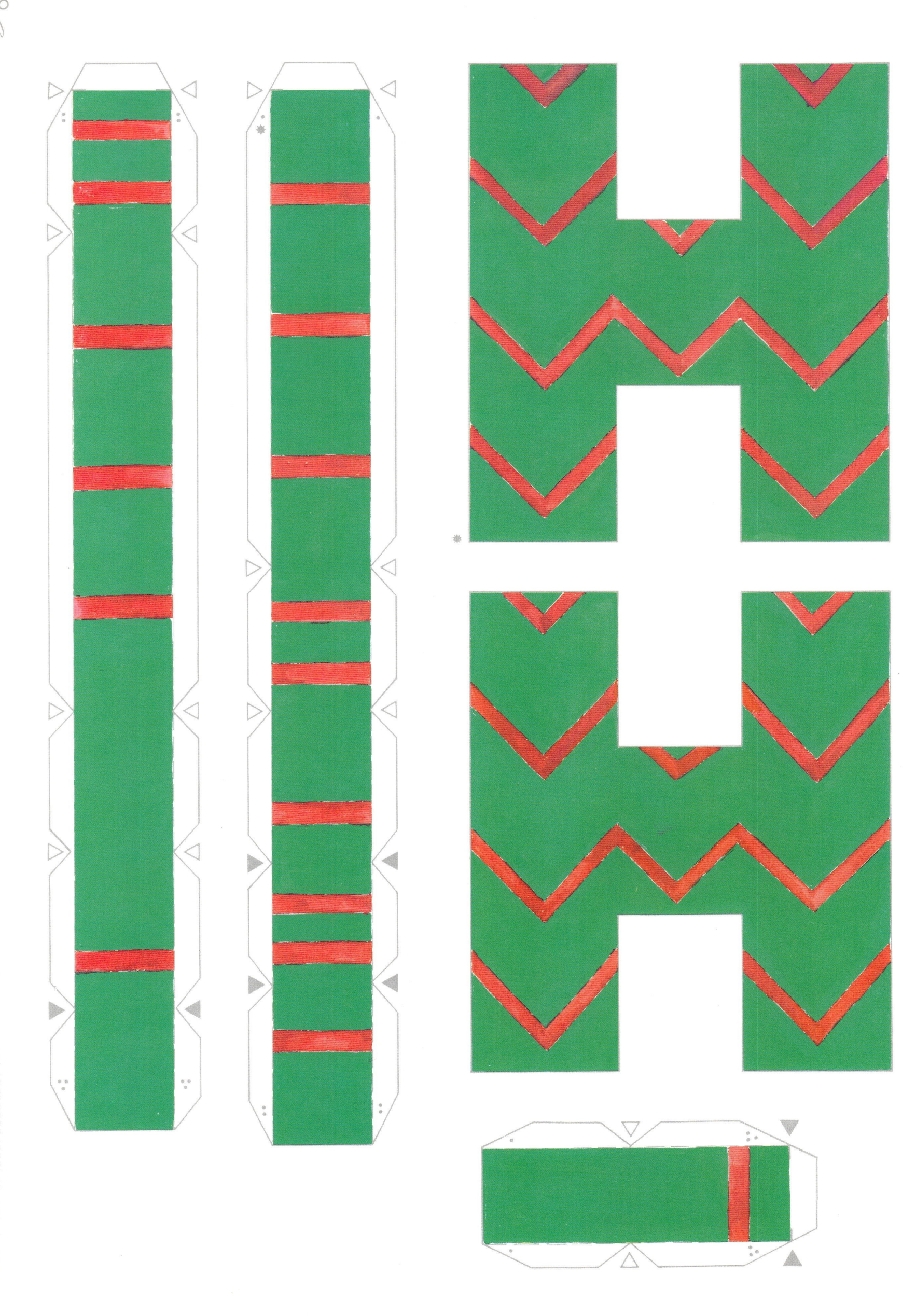

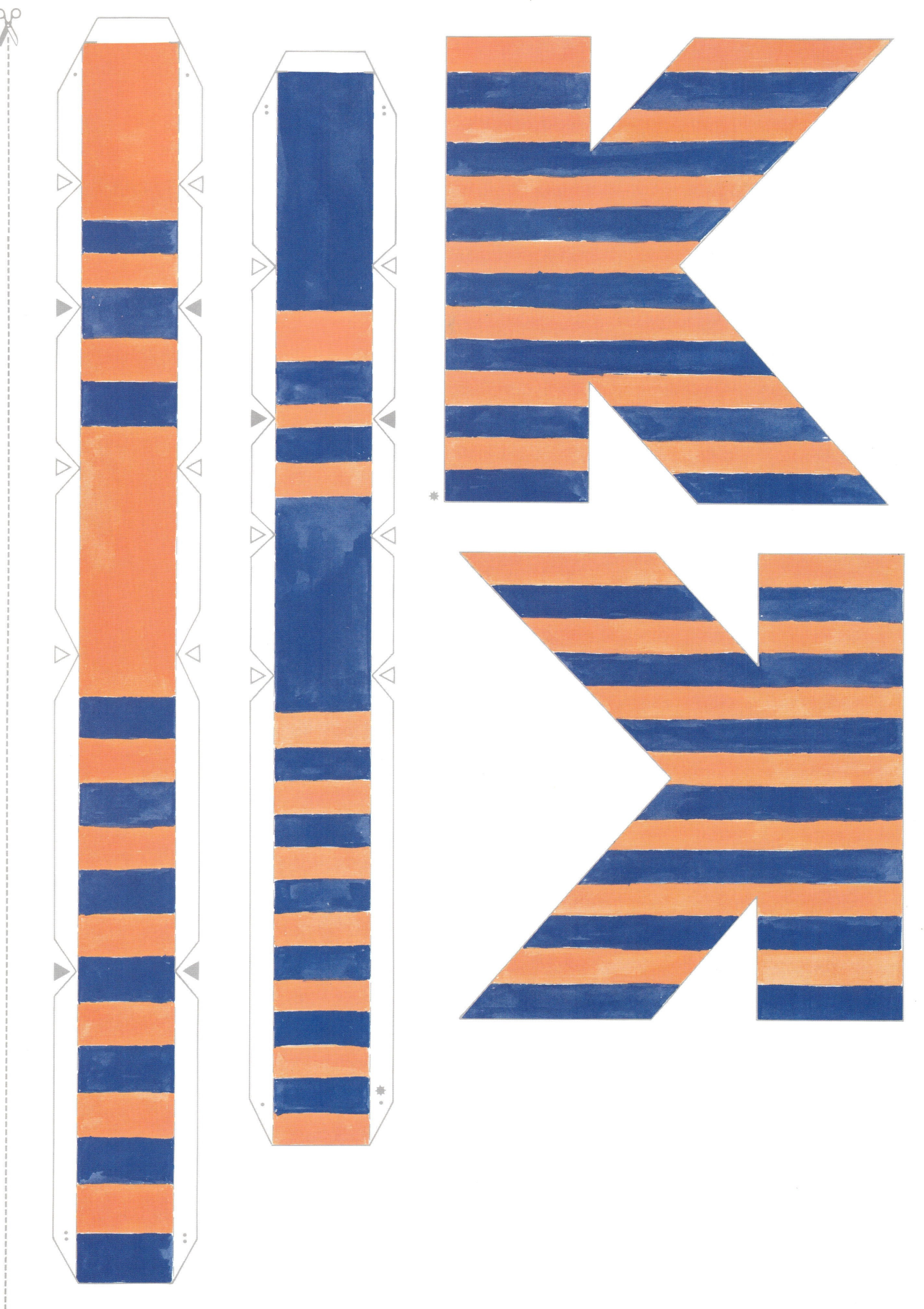

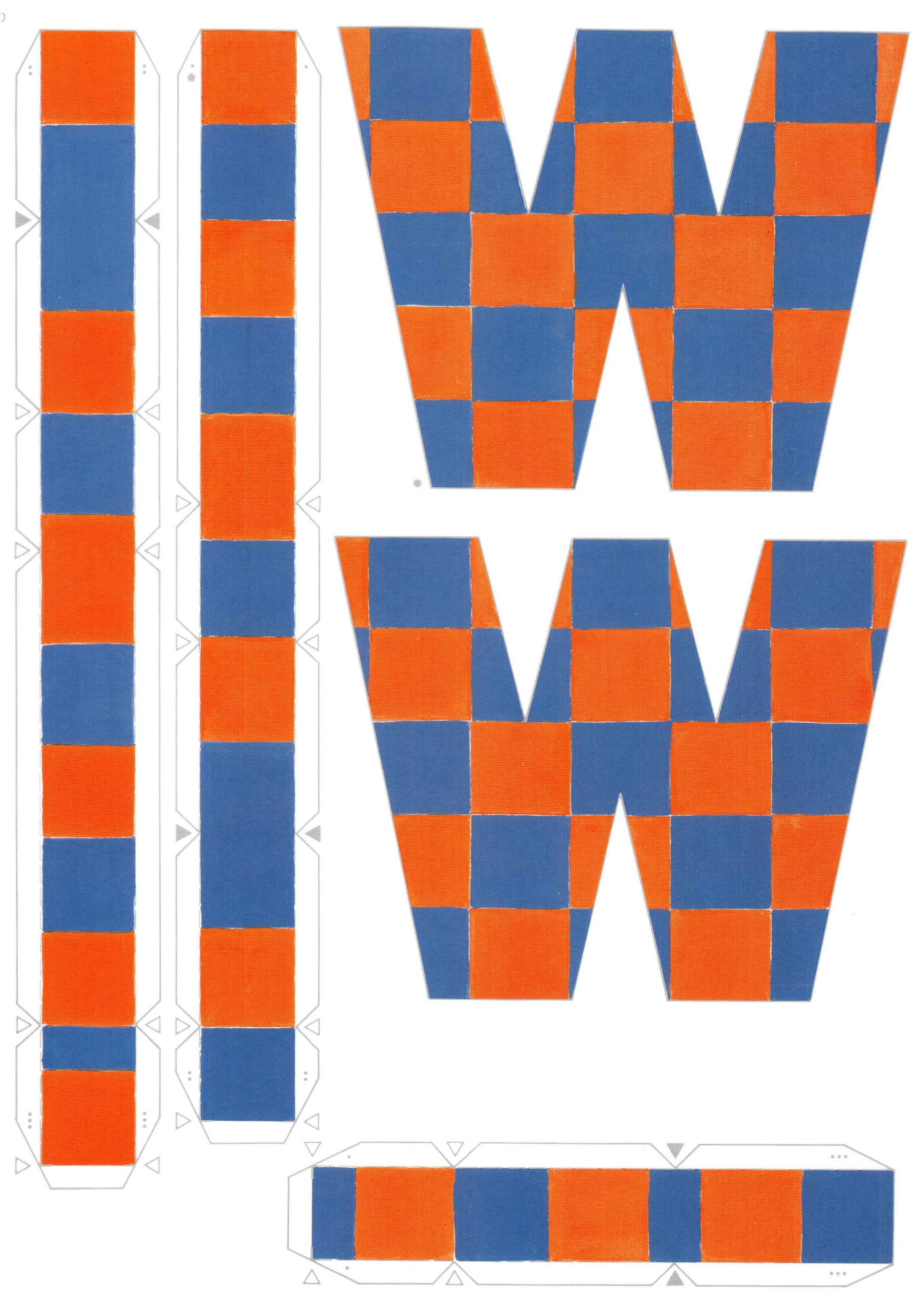

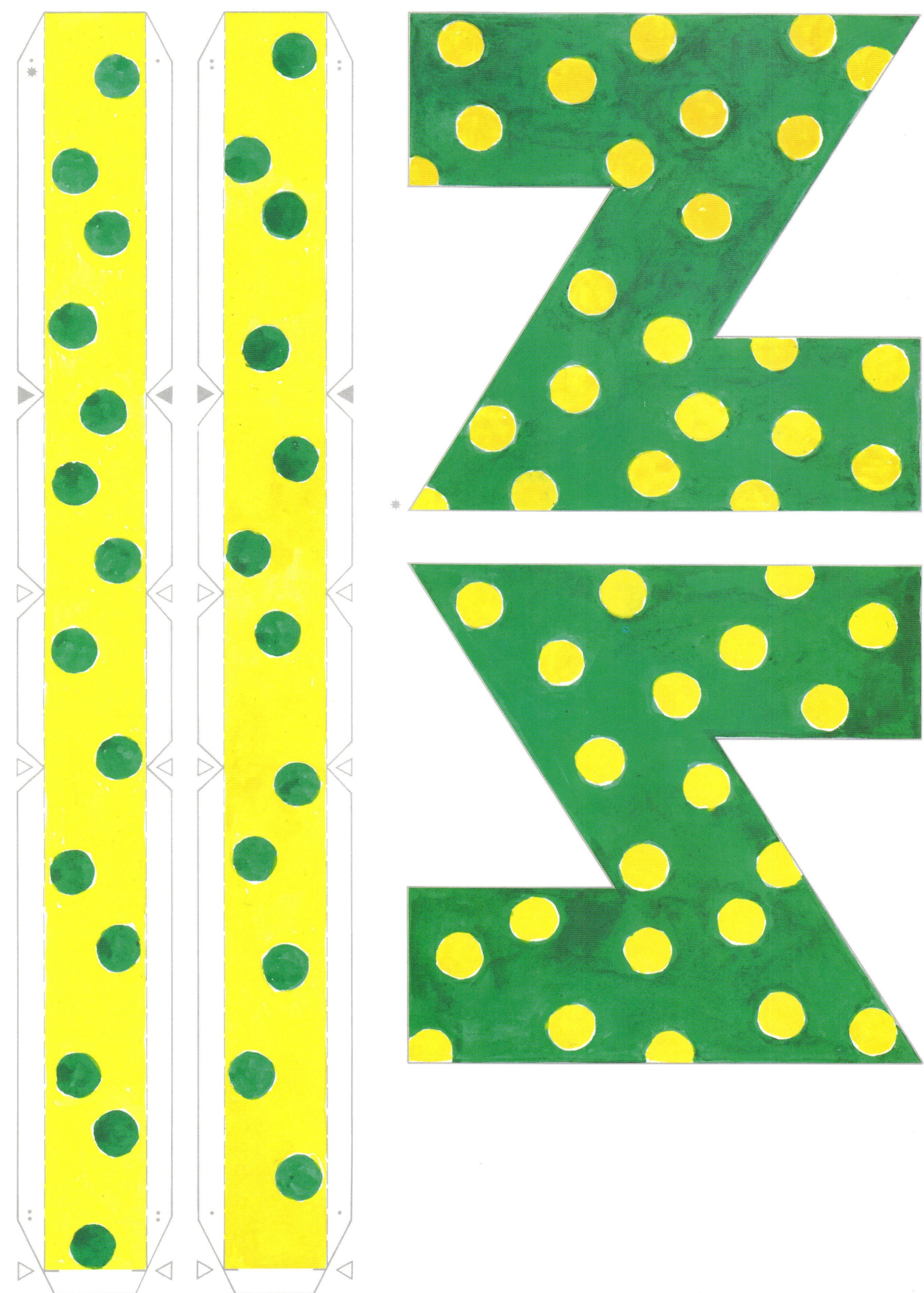

Editor: Margaret L. Kaplan
Concept and design by Joy Nagy
Alphabet by Caroline Mazzello

Library of Congress Cataloging-in-Publication Data
Nagy, Joy, 1940–
Build your own alphabet / by Joy Nagy.
   p. cm.
"A Regina Ryan book."
Summary: Colored, graphically designed patterns for each letter of the alphabet, which may be cut out and formed into five-inch high, five-inch wide, one-inch deep paper sculptures for learning, play, or decoration.
ISBN 0-8109-2416-1 (pbk.)
1. Paper work. 2. Alphabet. [1. Handicraft. 2. Initials.
3. Alphabet.] I. Title.
TT870.N25 1989
736'.98—dc19
[E]   88-27498

Copyright © 1989 Joy Nagy
Published in 1989 by Harry N. Abrams, Incorporated, New York
All rights reserved. No part of the contents of this book may be reproduced without the written permission of the publisher
A Times Mirror Company
Printed and bound in Japan